This journal belongs to:

_____

"Never, ever, let anyone tell you what you can and can't do. Prove the cynics wrong. Pity them, for they have no imagination. The sky's the limit. Your sky. Your limit. Now. Let's dance."

"What's my guilty pleasure?
The thing is I never feel
guilty about pleasures."

"Haters never win. I just think that's true about life, because negative energy always costs in the end."

"My advice is 'love your life'...
because your life is what
you have to give."

"You never know what's around the corner. It could be everything or it could be nothing. You keep putting one foot in front of the other. And then one day you look back and you've climbed a mountain."

"I never get afraid of things.
I only get excited."

"For myself, for a long time... Maybe I felt inauthentic or something, I felt like my voice wasn't worth hearing, and I think everyone's voice is worth hearing. So if you've got something to say, say it from the rooftops."

"Never stop.
Never stop fighting.
Never stop dreaming."

"I don't think anyone, until their soul leaves their body, is past the point of no return."

"Life is generally pretty damn amazing if you let it be."

"Every day is a creative act:
a step closer to becoming who
you want to be."

"I find that the only opinion that should matter is yours."

"Know that whatever bullies say or do, it comes from their weakness, not yours. The best revenge against bullies is absolutely, resolutely, never to let them change who you are."

"Responsibility is power. Take
responsibility for the consequences
of your actions, and the world is yours.
Everything is a choice."

"There is a lot of darkness in our world; there is a lot of pain, and you can either choose to see that or you can choose to see the joy. If you try to respond positively to the world, you'll spend your time better."

"If you risk failure, then
you also risk success."

"Dance more, smile more, tell lots
of jokes, and enjoy yourself.
That's the key."

"Every villain is a hero
in his own mind."

"We all have two lives.
The second one starts when
we realize that we only have one."

"Stay hungry, stay young, stay foolish, stay curious, and above all, stay humble because just when you think you got all the answers, is the moment when some bitter twist of fate in the universe will remind you that you very much don't."

"Everything's a choice.
Nobody's born good.
Nobody's born evil.
It's always a choice."

"I try not to make plans. God always laughs at your plans. I'm going to keep the door open, and keep the page blank, and see what gets painted upon it."

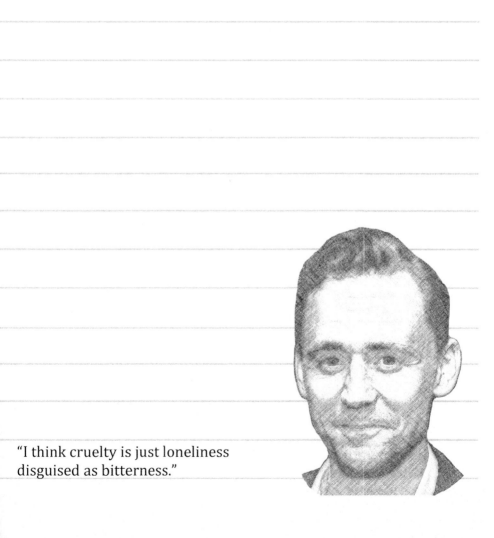

"I think cruelty is just loneliness
disguised as bitterness."

"Don't be afraid of wearing your heart on your sleeve - in declaring the films that you love, the films that you want to make, the life that you've had, and the lives you can help reflect in cinema."

"I gave myself permission to care, because there are a lot of people in this world who are afraid of caring, who are afraid of showing they care because it's uncool."

"Don't be afraid of your passion, give it free reign, and be honest and work hard and it will all turn out just fine."

"Within us there is the capacity
of being anyone or anything."

"People love escapism and there should be a place for it."

"Artists instinctively want to reflect humanity, their own and each other's, in all its intermittent virtue and vitality, frailty and fallibility."

"I feel as though the cardboard box of my own reality has been flattened and blown open. Now I can see the edge of the world."

"It's in our nature to want to watch our human frailties played out on a huge, epic canvas. Ancient societies had anthropomorphic gods: a huge pantheon expanding into centuries of dynastic drama: fathers and sons, star-crossed lovers, warring brothers, martyred heroes. Tales that taught us the danger of hubris and the primacy of humility. It's the everyday stuff of everyman's life, but it's writ large, and we love it."

"The thing that keeps you grounded is doing the thing you love."

"Somehow the past is a safe place
to explore our collective
cultural neuroses."

"Nurture your own confidence
and make it real; don't pretend
to be someone you're not."

"The dream is to keep surprising
yourself, never mind the audience."

"Maybe it's just getting older. You become so palpably aware this is not a dress rehearsal. There's a big sign in blazing neon that says you haven't got long. But I think it takes a beat to learn that. Life has to knock you down in order for you to realize it, because when you're a kid you think you're immortal."

"I enjoy not knowing where my
next job is coming from."

"I belong where there are mountains and snow and clear, crisp blue skies."

"In our increasingly secular society, with so many disparate gods and different faiths, superhero films present a unique canvas upon which our shared hopes, dreams, and apocalyptic nightmares can be projected and played out."

"I grew up watching *Superman*.
As a child, when I first learned to
dive into a swimming pool, I wasn't
diving, I was flying, like superman.
I used to dream of rescuing a girl I had
a crush on from a playground bully."

"For me, love is about acceptance, and I think there's a sonnet which describes it perfectly: 'Love is not love which alters when it alteration finds.' To me that sums up love. It's constant and it doesn't change with the wind."

"I don't want to look back and go,
"God, I wish I'd done all of this
stuff that I've always wanted to do."

Printed in Great Britain
by Amazon

24443991R00066